A DRY ROOF
AND A COW

*To commemorate 75 years of service
in the name of Christ*

1 9 2 0 – 1 9 9 5

A DRY ROOF AND A COW

DREAMS AND PORTRAITS OF OUR NEIGHBOURS

Edited by Howard Zehr and Charmayne Denlinger Brubaker
Designed by Judith Rempel Smucker

A MENNONITE CENTRAL COMMITTEE PUBLICATION
AKRON, PENNSYLVANIA • WINNIPEG, MANITOBA

C O N T E N T S

FOREWORD

For most people and most organizations, the commemoration of an anniversary is relatively straightforward.

We at Mennonite Central Committee decided that for us celebrating 75 years of service was not enough; we also wanted to reflect on what it will mean to serve others "In the Name of Christ" in the next decades and to call others to join us in a recommitment to that service. We were sure that stories of triumphal successes from 1920 to 1995 ill fitted an agency whose major mission has been to respond to pain and suffering. We were also sure that as representatives of the Mennonite, Brethren in Christ and Amish churches, we ought to emphasize the empowerment that comes from a compassionate, concerned peoplehood rather than organizational achievement.

The primary clue for our celebration comes through the reflections of 10,000 volunteer workers who have served God by serving others during these 75 years. All Mennonite Central Committee workers I know, without exception, say that they have learned far more during their months and years of service than they may have contributed to ameliorating the human condition. Given this sentiment, we decided the most authentic celebration would be rooted in gratitude.

We believe the best way to say thank you is to highlight the aspirations, hopes and dreams of our neighbours from around the world. The quotations recorded in this book suggest that their hopes and dreams are almost too obvious in their simplicity—for a dry shelter, for sufficient food, for freedom to walk the streets without fear. Responding to these aspirations has guided Mennonite Central Committee since its beginning in 1920.

We also say thank you for God's grace and call and thank you to congregations and families who nurtured and encouraged this ministry; above all, thank you to churches and communities who have given us an opportunity to serve "In the Name of Christ."

Mennonite Central Committee is grateful to those who created this book: the seven photographers, the three writers, the editor and designer, the printers.

We urge each reader to ponder the strength and dignity of the people portrayed here, to reflect on the hopes and dreams of these friends. We invite you to join us in saying thank you, to join again God's concern for the well-being of all people.

John A. Lapp
Executive Secretary
Mennonite Central Committee

INTRODUCTION

This is a book of faces, human faces from Bangladesh, British Columbia, Vietnam, West Bank, Bolivia, Florida and Burkina Faso. They are all marked by pain as well as hope. They all express unspeakable sorrow as well as unshakable joy. They all reflect the great mystery that fear and love, despair and hope, doubt and trust, are never separated in the human heart.

Those who have the inner courage to give time and attention to the people who are portrayed in this book, and to their penetrating words, will gradually discover the blessings of the poor. All the faces who look at us from these pages are faces of people suffering from poverty, whether caused by oppression, violence, hunger, loss of identity, lack of education or by any other form of discrimination. They are marginalized men and women, victims of gross injustice. Still... they all have dreams, they all speak of hope, they all look beyond their own pain to a new future.

Jesus did not say: "Blessed are those who care for the poor," but "Blessed are the poor."

The blessing—that is encouragement, hope and healing—is hidden in those who stand on the margins of our society. They may not be successful, powerful or famous, but they have the unique ability to call us, who stand in the centre, to the truth. It is so easy to forget that we are all daughters and sons of the same God, that all divisions and separations between people are human-made, and that we are all called to live the short journey from birth to death with justice and in peace. We, who live in the centre, are so busy planning our lives and controlling others' lives that we have become deaf to the voice that calls us beyond our own and other people's lives, into the mystery of God's eternal love.

Those who stand on the margins of our society, who have little to control, and wonder how to make it through another day, another week or another year, are our true prophets. In their vulnerability and weakness they force us to question the foundation of our security. When Jesus, "the marginal Jew," said to James and John, "Come, follow me," they immediately left their nets and their family, and followed him (Mark 1:15–20). "Nets" is economic security and "family," emotional security. Those on the margins of our society are often without nets or family. Their hope in a future cannot be based on money in the bank or good connections. Their hope has to be based on love, a love that is real, personal and intimate, a love that is stronger than death, a love that is called God.

As proclaimers of that love they bring a blessing. The world needs that blessing more than ever, because with our increased defense capabilities, through military technology, any form of separation or division among people could be fatal for the survival of humanity.

Let's explore this blessing a little more. As I look at the faces in this book and read the words that accompany them, I realize that these men and women are standing under the cross, as the mother of Jesus stood there, saying, "We trust that our suffering will bear fruit." Ousmane Ouedraogo trusts that one day he will have a secure home, even though he has seen many mud houses being washed away by rain. Ima Geries trusts that one day there will be a place where young men aren't afraid, even though her own son was killed by soldiers. Janet Powell trusts that her grandchildren will be proud of themselves and know their culture, even though she witnessed how her own people were robbed of their identity.

Rays of light are shining through the broken lives of these people. They are in touch with something larger than a wish for a gift from the stranger who might come along and show pity on them. They are in touch with a dream that makes them visionaries of a new future.

They trust their dream. As the first Joseph trusted his dreams and saved his people from starvation, as the second Joseph trusted his dream and took Mary as his wife and Jesus as his child, and as Martin Luther King, Jr., trusted his dream and led his people to new freedom, so also are these men and women full of trust that their dream will guide them to the fulfillment of the promise they carry in their hearts. Indeed, their dreams are, in the words of Filomena Saucedos Ame, "greener than a parrot."

A people without a dream dies. Without a dream there is no hope, and without hope there is no future. Without a future there is no one to care for but ourselves. The blessing we need so much is the blessing that lifts us out of our preoccupation with success, power and fame, and makes us look far beyond the horizon of our own little lives.

That blessing says, "You are greater than your fearful heart, you are loved deeper than your parents could ever love you, you are safer than any money can ever make you, you belong to God from eternity to eternity, and nothing created can ever take that away from you." That blessing restores our dream and makes us live with eyes open to a future full of light.

Does all of this mean that it is good to be poor or marginal? If the poor are blessed, is their condition to be envied? Is calling the poor "blessed" a dangerous romanticization of those in our world who lack the privileges we enjoy?

Cursed are those who think or act in such a manner! Only through a just distribution of the wealth of our world will peace and happiness among people be realized. The marginalized are marginal because those who do not want to leave the centre keep them at the margins. The blessing of the marginal is a blessing that empowers us to move out of the centre and cross all boundaries that keep us separated from other human beings. That blessing transcends all divisions between rich and poor, powerless and powerful, and re-establishes the truth that all people are brothers and sisters in the same human family.

That is what this book is about! As we allow the people who appear on these pages to look deeper into our hearts, and as we allow their words to penetrate our very souls, we will soon realize that they are born as we are born, sharing with us the human struggle, and will die as we will. They are humans as we are human, mortal as we are mortal, but eternally loved by the same God who gave life to us.

I trust that, as we let the words and images in this book penetrate our hearts, we will experience a deep desire to do whatever possible to make the dream of a worldwide community of love and peace become a reality.

Henri J. M. Nouwen
February 1994

HENRI J.M. NOUWEN is the author of more than 30 books including *With Open Hands, Return of the Prodigal Son, In the Name of Jesus* and *Compassion.* He has taught at the University of Notre Dame, South Bend, Indiana; Harvard Divinity School, Cambridge, Massachusetts; and Yale Divinity School, New Haven, Connecticut. He studied at the Menninger Clinic, Topeka, Kansas. He currently lives at Daybreak L'Arche, a community for people with mental handicaps and their assistants, located in Richmond Hill, Ontario.

FLORIDA

BELLE GLADE

by Dorothy Littell Greco

SONIA GUILLAUME

interviewing clerk at social services agency

"I would love to return to Haiti
if things get better there.

My hope for the Haitian community
here in Belle Glade is for them to
work together more,
and be a powerful community,
like the Cubans."

MAXO SAINT CLAIR

nursing student

"**F**irst my dream was to drive a big truck.

Now I am going to school
to be a patient care assistant.

If I have the opportunity to
bring my family here,
it would be better for me."

SAUVEUR PIERRE

legal services staff

"There are two things that I always think about:
to be a photographer or a dentist.

I am interested in doing things
where I meet a lot of people.

I am most interested in photography
because I can meet people
and do it on my own."

FRANTZ GAUDARD

college student,
tutor and language facilitator

"**M**y dream is to serve God.

Besides that,
probably to get married and have a family.
Maybe pursue a bachelor's degree
in electrical engineering,

but I still want to help with the kids."

DIEU DONNE AND LUNIE BRUTUS

storekeepers and pastor

"I would like to have only one business instead of two,
and to take care of my church.

If someone offered me anything I want, I'd say,
        'OK, now I am going to school to study English
        and to do something good for my mind
        and to help people know Jesus.'"
—*Dieu*

"Yes, that's my thing too."
—*Lunie*

WESLEY JEUDY

ninth grade student

"I would like to go to school so I could be a musician.

I know that I would need money
to go to law school,
so I could earn it being a musician.

Then maybe later I could go to law school."

MORALES ST. HILAIRE

pastor and government worker

"**H**aitians come here and cannot speak any English.
They cannot read or write.
They are helpless.
I don't see any future for their children.

My biggest dream is to see
Haitian kids have a good education.
This way, they can help others.

And I would like to have a church
where people could really support education."

MENNONITE CENTRAL COMMITTEE IN
BELLE GLADE
FLORIDA

In 1982 the first Mennonite Central Committee volunteers went to Belle Glade, Florida, to provide health care and social services to Haitian farm workers in local sugar cane and vegetable fields. This ministry to some of the 12,000 Haitians living in and around the town was started at the invitation of Lutheran Ministries. Lutheran Ministries provided the funding; Mennonite Central Committee provided the volunteers.

Today Mennonite Central Committee's work in Belle Glade, Florida, still focuses on Haitians. Workers there teach English to Creole-speaking Haitians, serve in local housing projects and work in social work, peacemaking and ethnic reconciliation assignments. They also work closely with Tet Ansanm, a Haitian community group that leads after-school and summer youth programs. In 1994 for the first time a volunteer joined Centro Campesino, an agency that focuses on migrant farm worker housing problems.

DOROTHY LITTELL GRECO is a freelance photographer and writer based in Boston, Massachusetts. She works for editorial and corporate clients, including the *Los Angeles Times, WGBH* and *Yankee Magazine,* and pursues documentary projects. She has had several solo exhibits and has twice won awards from Communications Arts and from the National Press Photographers' Association.

BANGLADESH

by Shahidul Alam

ELENA DIAZ

grandmother

"I don't really have any desires.

I would like to go to the Lord.
I would like a dry shelter."

MD. BELAYET HOSSAIN

agricultural worker

"In my dreams, I would like a cow."

HAJERA KHATOON

maker of handmade paper

"I pray for a home of my own,
that I do not want,
that I can eat,
have enough clothes to wear.

It is not enough to hope and pray.
This I ask of God and he does not reply."

NAZMUN NAHAR BEGUM

laundrywoman

"I have four daughters and have stopped
having children.
I would have liked to have had a son."

ROLAND GONZALVEZ

office manager

"The reality is I am from a simple Bangladeshi home.
So I will always have to work.

I am looking for job satisfaction—
to work in an environment that is peaceful,
where people get along
and don't exploit each other."

ALIA

servant

"I don't know how to read or write
so I want to marry a man who is educated."

NURUL HAQUE

guard and gardener

"I always want to be working.
That's when I am happiest."

MENNONITE CENTRAL COMMITTEE IN

BANGLADESH

SHAHIDUL ALAM lives and works in Dhaka, Bangladesh. He is founder and director of Drik Picture Library Limited, dedicated to "presenting images of the Third World by Third World photographers." Dr. Alam is also the principal founder of the Bangladesh Photographic Institute. Dr. Alam has traveled widely and is well known among documentary photographers. He recently received the prestigious Mother Jones International Fund for Documentary Photography award.

On November 12, 1970, a devastating cyclone with accompanying 10-meter tidal waves killed some 500,000 people in East Pakistan, now known as Bangladesh. Millions of others were injured and left homeless.

Mennonite Central Committee responded by sharing $35,000, a boat, several outboard motors, canned chicken and blankets. Two workers from Nepal went to Bangladesh to help distribute this aid.

In the months following, civil war engulfed Bangladesh, bringing even more suffering and pain to the people there. Mennonite Central Committee committed more resources—money and workers—to binding up the wounds of war.

In 1994 Mennonite Central Committee's ministry in Bangladesh included not only short-term relief after natural disasters but also agriculture development, land reclamation, health work and a 21-year-old job-creation emphasis. Creating jobs for poor rural families is one way Mennonite Central Committee is a Christian resource for meeting human need in Bangladesh, a country where at least half of the population is unemployed or underemployed.

BRITISH COLUMBIA

PORT HARDY

by David Neel

DOREY BROTCHIE

artist

"I would like my children to know they're strong—
to know their language, to know the history,
the background of both their mother and the father,
  then down the line
   to the grandfather, grandmother,
   the great-grandmother, the great-grandfather.

They already have Indian names.
This will give them something to be proud of."

AGNES PAUL

elder

"**Y**ears ago we used to go fishing together.
But with individual homes, everything changed.
Now we don't even say hello to our neighbours.

It would be nice to know everybody
who lives in the same area.
Maybe that's what is missing in this village:
there are no people getting together in their homes."

MARGARET COON *(right)*
WITH MARY WALKUS

day-care worker

"I want to go to college next year.
I want to be a cop,
because I don't see many Native police.

And I want to travel."

RAVENA SWAIN

student

"My dream is to either become a teacher
or a social worker.

If I had one wish, I would wish that
the reserve could become more peaceful
and free of alcohol and drugs.

That would open a lot of doors
for our community."

JOHN CHARLIE
elder

"I wish and pray for my children not to be changed,
to not change their way of living.

I used to listen to my grandfather:
     'You don't steal other people's things,
     not even their names.
     You keep your own.
     And when that guy there needs help,
     and you have things, you go and help them.'

I wish my grandchildren and my kids felt like that."

**RICHARD GEORGE
AND DAUGHTER SALINA**

counselor

"**A**ll I can do for my community and for my own family
is to be an example of what I've done in my own life.
We as individuals have good and we have bad,
and we have to make choices.

    For my little girl,
    the biggest dream that I have is for her
    to live in a healthy environment
    and to go through all her education.

    I share with her in my healing journey
    and don't hide anything from her.
And I keep acknowledging to her that I have a lot of love
for her grandma and grandpa and her uncles and cousins."

JANET POWELL AND SON JAMES

retired health and welfare counselor

"I just hope I'll be around long enough to see
         my grandchildren grow up
         and know who they are,
         to be proud of themselves
         and know their culture.

         That's what's wrong with a lot of people today:
         they've lost their identity.

I listened to all my ancestors
         and that's what I tried to teach
         my children and grandchildren."

PORT HARDY

BRITISH COLUMBIA

DAVID NEEL is a professional photographer and hereditary artist in the Kwagiutl wood-carving and painting tradition. He works in a number of mediums including printmaking and precious metals. He writes and lectures about art and Native issues in Canada. After studying in Kansas and Texas, he returned to Canada, where he lives with his wife and their five children in Campbell River, British Columbia. His work is exhibited internationally and he has received numerous grants and awards for his documentary-style work. He is currently working on a book about the Northwest coast dugout canoe, and his book *Our Chiefs and Elders* (Neel, UBC Press, Vancouver, British Columbia and University of Washington Press, Seattle, Washington), which combines portraits and words from First Nations leaders, is being released in paperback.

In the early 1960s two isolated communities of the Gwa'Sala and Nakwaxda'xw people were relocated to a small reserve adjacent to the village of Port Hardy on Vancouver Island. Houses on the traditional village sites were then burned by government agents to ensure the people would not return. When the Gwa'Sala and Nakwaxda'xw communities arrived at the new location, few houses were available and numerous families were compelled to live on their fishing boats, thus forfeiting a livelihood. Despair eventually resulted and social problems became endemic.

In 1974 two Mennonite Central Committee workers went to Port Hardy to provide a quiet Mennonite presence, to seek to understand the complex situation and to explore ways of working with the people on issues they defined.

Since then Mennonite Central Committee has had a continuous presence with the Gwa'Sala and Nakwaxda'xw people working together on such varied projects as a group home, employment and a school. Volunteers have a remarkable friendship with the community, and a local Mennonite fellowship has resulted.

BOLIVIA

by Jon Warren

EUSEBIO CARRASCO
WITH SON MARCO ANTONIO

farmer and peasant union leader

"**M**y parents did not know how to improve their situation,
for example by a system of cultivating citrus fruits.

I want to improve what I have
and leave an example for my family.

I want to organize groups for projects and financing.
If we peasants don't come together,
then we will go on living the way we do now,
as peasants."

CLARA RODRÍGUEZ RICO

bread and candle maker

"I ask God to help me improve my business
to save some money.
But my greatest wish would be
to have my own house.
You suffer a lot if you don't have
your own home.

For the community,
I wish that this area would receive plumbing."

**FILOMENA SAUCEDOS AME
AND CLEMENTE SALAS SAUCEDOS**

mother; farmer and church leader

"**W**e, the sisters of the Mennonite church,
have a prayer meeting on Thursdays.
We pray and plan.
Our mission now is to add two or more rooms in the church
so there will be enough space.

Some sisters say this dream is
          'greener than a parrot'—
          that is, that's too much hope—
but we have to have confidence
that the Lord can do everything and will help us.

We don't have much,
but we have hope in our God."
—*Filomena*

"Some of my children still do not know the Lord.
          What would happen if the Lord came
          and found them without having repented?

          I always live with that tragedy
          and pray and ask our Saviour to
          change their attitude
          so that they may understand that
only through the Lord can we find our salvation."
—*Clemente*

**ANGELA HURTADO
WITH DAUGHTER BEVERLY**

homemaker

"Oh, the dreams that people dream:
　　　I'm always dreaming of good things.

　　　My one wish would be
　　　that in my home I could be an example
　　　to my children, to my husband,
　　　so that we could have a better life.

I pray that the Lord may guide us
and help us move ahead."

PABLO MOYA
ALEJANDRO PARRA
ROLY CALDERÓN

children's home residents

"I want to be a doctor in the United States.
I want to help poor people."
—*Pablo, 14*

"If I had a magic lamp,
I'd ask for a house in the city with
three bathrooms, a big living room,
four bedrooms, a game and music room!"
—*Alejandro, 14*

"I want to study at the university
to be a veterinarian."
—*Roly, 13*

LINO CARRASCO

metal and appropriate technology worker

"I want to have my own metal workshop.
Then I want to get married.

But first I want to get a house.
That is my most important dream:
a normal house in the country
with one or two rooms."

SOFÍA CHAO

chairperson for national group,
subsistence hunter, gatherer, farmer

"I like living by the road instead of in the jungle.

What do I want to have?
Clothes, knives, shovels, axes, animals, chickens!

And I want to live long enough
to see my great-grandchild born."

MENNONITE CENTRAL COMMITTEE IN
BOLIVIA

Mennonite Central Committee service with Bolivians started in 1962 when the Methodist Church there invited Mennonite workers to serve in an integrated community development program among Altiplano Indians. In following years Mennonite Central Committee's ministry broadened to include appropriate technology, holistic farming systems and social and medical services.

Today Mennonite Central Committee's 31 workers in Bolivia are in assignments such as housing, library programs for street children, job creation, appropriate technology, health education, sheep farming and water-source improvement.

JON WARREN specializes in international editorial and documentary photography. Born and raised in India, he has had assignments in more than 34 countries. His work appears in many publications including the 1992 book *Celebrate, The God Who Loves* (Warren, SIM, Scarborough, Ontario), a pictorial of people and religion around the world. Warren has received awards from Communications Arts, Pictures of the Year, National Press Photographers' Association and The Evangelical Press Association and has had several solo exhibits.

MENNONITE COLONIES

BOLIVIA

by Jon Warren

**HELENA KROEKER
WITH SONS NORMAN
AND EDWARD**

homemaker

"Looking into the future is a luxury I can't afford.
It is too frightening.

I can look only a few steps ahead
and hope I'm still able to walk

and that my sons will find
small tokens of acceptance."

*Helena Kroeker has chronic back problems and two
handicapped sons.*

FRANZ FEHR

metal worker

"**M**y desire would be to develop
a comfortable farming operation within
the present structures of our colony."

**KATHARINA,
SUSANNA AND
MARGARETHA LOEWEN**

"When I'm grown up
I'd like to wash dishes and clean up for others.
I wish I could make a trip to Canada
and stay there among my relatives
and help them."
—*Katharina, 10*

"I think it would be easiest
to make a living like we do here,
living together and farming.
I'd like to get married
just like everyone else to someone
nice from our colonies.
The only wish I'd have is
that I'd be appropriate and worthy."
—*Susanna, 17*

"I would like something better
than what we have here.
At night I mostly think about my boyfriend.
In 10 years I'd like to be with him,
making a living together.
If I had one wish it'd be
to get along with everyone."
—*Margaretha, 16*

JACOB REMPEL

farmer and welder

"I survived three years of debtors' prison
and problems of addiction.

My strong desire is to
make a fresh, successful start
in establishing my own home,
working my own soil
and being true to
a new commitment to God."

**GERHARD SIEMENS
WITH WIFE SUZANNA**

rug and fence maker

"**O**f course, I would like to walk again.

I would like to set up a store;
I am a businessman at heart
and like to make deals."

*Gerhard Siemens was wounded in a robbery
at his brother's store.*

LISA NEUFELD

nurse

"**M**y dream is that we,
 as a family,
 and as a colony and church,
          could go beyond
          mere form
          and really live out the call
          to a Christian life."

DAVID REMPEL

farmer, about to be married

"My main wish is that
my life would be like Jesus Christ's
and that I will love my wife.

I see many families without love
and I don't like that."

MENNONITE CENTRAL COMMITTEE IN

BOLIVIA
MENNONITE COLONIES

JON WARREN specializes in international editorial and documentary photography. Born and raised in India, he has had assignments in more than 34 countries. His work appears in many publications including the 1992 book *Celebrate, The God Who Loves* (Warren, SIM, Scarborough, Ontario), a pictorial of people and religion around the world. Warren has received awards from Communications Arts, Pictures of the Year, National Press Photographers' Association and The Evangelical Press Association and has had several solo exhibits.

Mennonite Central Committee first went to Bolivia in 1959 to assist Mennonite colonists from Paraguay who were trying to farm east of Santa Cruz in Tres Palmas. These families needed not only agricultural assistance, but also medical services and health education. Mennonite Central Committee workers also helped these families secure loans for their agricultural operations. In 1960 a Mennonite Central Committee nurse started a small clinic in Tres Palmas, providing inoculations, routine health care and emergency and maternity services. The clinic served native Bolivians as well as colonists.

Today Centro Menno in Santa Cruz, Bolivia, is a hub of activity for Bolivia Colony Mennonites. Staff at the centre provide medicines; in a literacy program, they provide German reading material to teachers and children. Centre staff help colonists who want to move to new colonies due to crowded conditions in the current colonies; they also help colonists prepare the legal documents needed to move to Canada.

WEST BANK

by Howard Zehr

MONA DUZDAR

clerk and office assistant

"I wish, truly, from my heart,
not to be wealthy,
not for money,
        but to do something to help
        poor and needy people.

        And I wish
all people could go back to God—
he asks us to love each other.

People here don't need peace.
They need justice.
If there is justice,
peace will come afterward."

IMA GERIES

retired school cook

"After my son was killed
by soldiers,
my heart is no longer in anything.

I don't want anything;
I am discouraged from life.

How can I live
with my enemy
after what they have done?

But I still hope for peace—
the kind of peace
where young men aren't afraid."

SULIEMAN NOUR

teacher

"**A**t Hope School, I think I achieved something.
I established the business courses
and I hope to see them going on.

As a Palestinian, my dream has been
just to live freely in my country.
To have our own independent state.
We just want to live free
with no occupation,
with no soldiers—
to have our own identity, our own freedom."

GEORGE JACOB AL-ATRASH

olive-wood craftsman

"**I** am very interested that my kids finish their studies
and get higher education.
We are teaching them at home, but we are very tired
of this situation.

We hope that one day there will be peace
and then our children will go to school regularly.

If I had one wish,
it would be to be free in our country,
not live all the time under threats and pressure.

To have land to build a house."

*At the time of the interview, George Al-Atrash was
banned from working because of tax resistance.*

FATHER MANUAL MUSSALAM

school principal

"I am 52 years old.
I passed through six, seven, eight wars
from 1938 until now.
        I was born in war.
Now we suffer the ninth war, with Iraq.

We hope that we will finish our life
without another war.
But it is too hard to imagine such a life here.
It is a spiral of violence.

        What do we hope?
        It is to have an idea of security.

        Peace is an unknown word here in this country.
Peace is something without any concept in the head.
Even when we try to ask our fathers or grandfathers,
        they have never passed through peace
        to tell us what is peace."

HANAN ATTALAH ISSA

nursing student

"**M**y hope is for every Palestinian to be free,
to feel that they are not treated worse
because they are Palestinian.

　　　　　And it is important for me in the long run
　　　　　to have a home of my own and a family of my own,
　　　　　but I don't put it as my first priority now.

　　　　　My first hope,
and I am determined to do it,
is to continue my education, to have my master's."

*Hanan Issa is a nursing student
whose family home in a refugee camp was demolished
by soldiers because her brother was suspected of
throwing stones.*

FIRAS ISSAC

student

"For 40 years, before the Intifada,
    there was nothing.
            But now we are living for something.

            My dream is to have the Israelis out of here,
            to live like other people and be able to
            enjoy life.

I like walking at night.
Now you can't.
            My two uncles and their friends were out
            and the Israelis took them and beat them
            for two hours and then released them,

            just for walking."

MENNONITE CENTRAL COMMITTEE IN THE
WEST BANK

HOWARD ZEHR photographs for Mennonite Central Committee and directs the Office of Crime and Justice for Mennonite Central Committee U.S. in Akron, Pennsylvania. He has taught and worked as a freelance photographer. His work has often been published and exhibited. A current documentary exhibit titled "The Meaning of Life" consists of portraits of and interviews with men and women serving life sentences without possibility of parole.

In 1950 the West Bank town of Jericho welcomed a Mennonite Central Committee relief team that came to serve Arab Palestine refugees forced from their homes in 1948 when Israel was created as a Jewish homeland. This team distributed food, clothing and blankets and opened a vocational training centre to teach shoemaking to refugees. Providing relief was again an important component of the group's work in 1967 when Israel occupied the West Bank of the Jordan River.

Today Mennonite Central Committee's work in the West Bank is characterized by peace and human rights education and activities. Mennonite Central Committee welcomes visitors to its Peace Resource Centre in Jerusalem. It also provides scholarships for Hope Secondary School students in Beit Jala, a school started by Mennonite Central Committee in 1962 and now run by a board of Arab Christians.

SELFHELP Crafts of the World, a non-profit program of Mennonite Central Committee, provides fair, vital income to Third World people by marketing their handicrafts and telling their stories in North America. It markets olive wood and mother-of-pearl creations and intricate needlework crafted by Palestinian producers.

VIETNAM

by Leah Melnick

DO THI KIM NGAN

social worker,
job creation project

"**W**e found that the reason the children drop out of school
is because they need to find a job—
            they have no money.
Now we have a shop where most of the things
are made by children and other jobless people.

You at MCC show your love
not by saying but by doing, by encouraging;

you don't just say,
            'I love you, God loves you.'
            People understand,
            and that's what I hope other people will do
            when they work with our shop.
            The children don't need to hear
            'I love you;'
they need the encouragement
and understanding and action."

TRAN THI SAU

university English teacher

"During the war my parents' village was bombed.
I'm afraid of bombs.

My dreams didn't come true
so I stopped dreaming.
If you dream, you get headaches.

Now the situation is getting better
and I feel more hopeful.
I want to study medicine and to improve my English.
I hope my son will become a priest
and my daughter will be a pianist."

NGUYEN CAM LY

high school student

"**M**y dream is to pass the university entrance exams
and then work as an interpreter.
    I want to go far away,
    to change places,
    to know more about the world.

Vietnam is a poor country but I am hopeful.
I want to contribute part of my life
to my country to make it better.
    I hope the world will have no war,
    especially in Vietnam.

If we look to the past, we are sometimes afraid.
If we look to the future, I am hopeful."

*Nguyen Cam Ly is now studying at a university
in Toronto, Ontario.*

NGUYEN NGOC CHAU

retired gardener

"I wish I could contribute more to other people;
I'd like to improve the life of the people
in this home for poor old people.

    But my life is meaningless
    because I cannot contribute anything.

    I'm ashamed to visit my relatives
because even though I have hands and feet,
I have to live on the support of others.
I cannot support myself
and have to rely on the government."

DINH THI DONG

farmer and president,
village women's union

"**M**y children's life is better than mine
because they went to school.
All my children have finished high school
but I wish they had finished university education.

I have a plan for my grandchildren—
to study for higher levels than my children did.
I am old, 50, so the future is
my children and grandchildren.

But when I look at my life,
what I like the most are the rights of
freedom, democracy and self-decision.
We make our own decisions and do our own work
for a better life.

We are not ruled by another country."

FATHER PHAN KHAC TU

Catholic priest

"In our country, Catholics are a minority
and Buddhists are a majority,
        and they don't work together.

        My dream is for all religions in Vietnam
        to seek together and to be concerned with the
        same issues for the sake of the people.

        I have struggled
for the right of freedom of religion
and for no discrimination
between Catholics and Buddhists."

DO HONG NGOC

pediatrician and director,
city health and education centre

"**M**y daughter died in an accident
when she was going to do volunteer social work.

After she died,
I was so sad that I promised to use my skills to
change things for the benefit of my young medical students.
I hope in the future there will be
something better for them."

MENNONITE CENTRAL COMMITTEE IN
V I E T N A M

LEAH MELNICK of Northhampton, Massachusetts, is currently based in Thailand and Cambodia. Having received a master's degree from Hampshire College, Amherst, Massachusetts, she also teaches at the Arts Institute of Boston, Massachusetts. She has received numerous grants and fellowships and has been widely exhibited. Her work has been published or reviewed in *The Washington Post, The New York Magazine, Christian Science Monitor, Life* and other national periodicals.

In 1954 Mennonite Central Committee became the first North American Protestant relief agency to enter Vietnam, only months after the defeat of the French by the Vietnamese nationalists. Mennonite Central Committee volunteers distributed clothing, Christmas bundles, soap, food and school supplies to refugees from the north. At the invitation of church leaders and the Saigon-based Republic of Vietnam, Mennonite Central Committee began medical work.

In 1990 Mennonite Central Committee was again the first North American agency invited to re-open an office in Vietnam, 15 years after the end of the Vietnam War. Vietnamese officials cited Mennonite Central Committee's long history in the country as a major factor in their granting the Mennonites permission to again live and serve in the country. In the intervening years, Mennonite Central Committee's tree-planting, agriculture, health and education programs in Vietnam had been administered from Thailand.

Today Mennonite Central Committee work includes training primary health care workers, supporting a vocational agricultural training program and helping print high quality English-teaching textbooks. Mennonite Central Committee also supports students and teachers at various schools in Vietnam.

BURKINA FASO

by Mark Beach

JEANNE LALKOWANDE

student

"I would like to stay here and be a teacher."

OUSMANE OUEDRAOGO

guard and yardman

"If I had the means, I would go
to the village and make a secure house.

Now we have one room
and everything is made of mud bricks
that deteriorate when it rains.
          If I had the money,
          I'd build a really nice house out of cement
          that could last for a long time.
          I'd retire there.

That would be really great."

SIBDOU OUABA

community health worker

"I have hope because the situation is improving.

In my work as a health promoter,
I can see in the villages that there are babies
who are alive who might have died.
　　　　There are women who are really happy
　　　　because they have found help for their own
　　　　life situations.

I hope that in the next few years,
more problems can be resolved."

PEGUEWENDE SAWADOGO

university student

"After my studies in France, I want to come back
to work in this country,
to do something with young offenders
or with street children who haven't been in prison yet.

My dream is to start a
victim-offender reconciliation program,
to adapt the idea to the African context.
There is already something like that
in African village culture and I want to learn of it.

I have to go step by step."

KARIM PASSOULE

teacher

"When I was in primary school, I admired my teachers.
I asked myself why they were so generous
to give us their knowledge.

   Now I'm a teacher.
   My ambition is to perfect, to strengthen
   the knowledge I have, to acquire the techniques
   to transmit this in an effective way.

I would like to be called a magician.
Sometimes students say,
   'Is this so simple? Last year I understood nothing.'

   So they think there is magic in
   transmitting knowledge."

DJOUREMIKO JOB HIEN ("PAPA JOB")

church leader and retired shopkeeper

"**M**y hope is that the church will grow.

When the church started, we were few in number.
We bought a piece of land to build a church.
I said to the missionary,
  'Since the plot has space,
  we should make it bigger.'

He asked, 'Will the church be filled?'
  Then he went home to Switzerland
  and when he returned I said,

  'See!
  Even with two services,
  the church is filled each time.'"

DA SIE POUOR (PAUL)

community development worker

"I don't know whether there is
much future in mechanics for me,
but my vision is to understand very well how to make
earthen dams, to bring about development.
        I'd like to do research for development.

        If God calls me,
        I will go to help other countries.
        But I'd really rather help in the development
        of my own country.

But everything depends on God's plan."

MENNONITE CENTRAL COMMITTEE IN

BURKINA FASO

MARK BEACH of Washington, D.C., is a journalist and documentary photographer who has traveled widely, including a six-month stint in South Africa. After serving as filmmaker and photographer for Mennonite Central Committee, he worked as photographer and writer for a Lancaster, Pennsylvania, newspaper. He recently completed a master's degree in international journalism from Baylor University in Waco, Texas. He has had a number of solo exhibits and grants.

In 1975 Mennonite Central Committee was invited by the Alliance churches and missions to start a program in Upper Volta, now known as Burkina Faso. Water development projects accompanied by agricultural programs were top priorities. Program goals included training for building hand-dug wells and small dams and appropriate technology education.

Today Mennonite Central Committee's ministry in Burkina Faso includes planting medicinal trees and encouraging village artists to create dramas to teach village cooperation and to raise money to buy food for community work days. Mennonite Central Committee's work in the countryside revolves around encouraging people to build small water-retention levees and create seasonal ponds to collect water for animal and household use. Through its Global Family program in Burkina Faso, Mennonite Central Committee has assisted women and children widowed and orphaned by AIDS.

In my dreams I would like a cow.
Inside my brick house I and my family
will look up from our bowls and listen
to her low contented music after milking.

THE DREAM MOVEMENT

A close relative living in south Russia before World War I carried a dream throughout his childhood and young adulthood of some day wearing real leather shoes. As the son of lower-class Mennonites, he wore *Schlorre*, a wooden sole with a leather strap over the toes, or he went barefoot.

Several times in his youth shoes were nearly within his ability to purchase, only to elude him. After the war, he returned home with real army boots, for he had served as a medic with the Russian Red Cross for four years. But he had to give up his shiny leather boots at knifepoint to an anarchist during the Russian Revolution. Once again he wore the lowly wooden-soled sandal.

Shoes for this relative, Katie's father and Christine's grandfather, represented much more than foot protection. Shoes symbolized having a name, an identity, a place in the world. For him the dream of shoes was a dream of being, of finding justice in a world where the rich were very rich and the poor were very poor. And that dream carried him forward long after he wore shoes and was living in Canada.

How little we understand about dreams and their power to shape, to guide, to draw, even to subvert and conquer. Yes, admittedly, sometimes a dream is fuzzy and ethereal. Yet that should not deter us from reaching for the strength of dreams, for, as Shaemas O'Sheel writes, the person possessed by a dream knows "no more of doubting, . . . And never comes darkness down, but he greeteth a million morns."

That is what this book is about—real people possessed by real dreams in real time. Though they may live in the dark uncertainty of political unrest and oppression, poverty and homelessness, and other cruel injustices, they greet a million morns because they have a dream. These people are members of the dream movement, sometimes more powerful than armies and their weaponry.

Human beings must dream. Without dreams, there is no tomorrow, only death and hopelessness. The Israelites, newly released from Egyptian slavery, roamed the wilderness for 40 years with the dream of a place of their own, the Promised Land, lived in community with a covenanting God. Even today the dream-terms "Canaan" and "Beulah-land" are symbols of hope and freedom from bonds for thousands of people.

Gandhi, the great leader of a dream for home rule for India through peaceful nonresistance, once said that violence is "the law of the brute." If violence is the law of the brute, then peace and love also have their patterns, their rhythms, their rules, governing those who choose to dream of peace on earth according to God's designs.

What are these rhythms and rules that govern this dream movement?

• *The origin of dreams of peace and justice is struggle and pain.*

Theologian Dorothy Soelle writes, "Struggle is the source of hope. There is no hope without struggle" (*To Work and to Love*, Fortress). People outside the centres of power, who live on the underside of life, pushed down, set aside, waiting in refugee camps, in temporary homes in a war zone, in hiding in a cornfield or broken-down building, dream more. They know what is missing in their lives to make them whole.

A dream cannot be bought or sold on the marketplace like an electric toaster or a sloganed T-shirt, although modern advertising tempts consumers to believe they can purchase power, prestige and self-confidence on bargain tables heaped high with colourful goods and in showrooms filled with shiny dream-machines. Dreams of enough for everyone, of life without terror and violence, of children growing to adulthood equipped to take their rightful place in society, originate where life is affected by pain.

Dreams such as these in this book direct our attention to the violent context from which they come. They point to tears, to waiting, to terror, to desperation and to loss of meaning. They point to the unjust relationships between peoples and nations. They tell us that justice has not come. There is much work to do.

> I kneel in the Protestant church
> praying for the past to return
> when Mother bent over our rice field,
> planting and pulling.
>
> Now the window implodes, explodes my prayer,
> Glass spears sing against the wooden floor.
> Evening cool steals under my skirt,
> Lights vanish across the city
> like a film reeling backwards.
>
> I pull my coat over my head
> and dream I am at home in the village.
> When the sun becomes a flower

Mother cooks our rice over the fire.
In the moonlight her shadow swings over the canals,
releasing the dark rush of water into the field from the reed
      baskets.

I wake. Lights drop from the sky
across the black city like angry stars.

• *Dreamers of peace and justice are prophets.*

Dreamers such as those whose dreams you have read here
speak the truth, cutting the darkness with light as sharp as a
surgeon's knife though their language is simple and direct.
Their dreams point beyond themselves to a greater vision.
The uncelebrated prophets in this book dream dreams of love,
of peace among warring peoples, of sufficient food and of
opportunities for education for children. Such dreams can
only come to fruition in a world that makes more sense, where
peace and justice are accepted as the vision of humanity.

A prophet speaks a message with the hope of recapturing
the good and the beautiful. To dream God's dream is to speak
prophetically of God's plans and purposes for humankind. It
is the same vision the psalmist writes of:

Love and faithfulness meet together;
righteousness and peace kiss each other (Psalm 85:10 NIV).

But a dream is also an honest, powerful judgement of an
unjust world, just like a stormy sea judges the unworthiness
of a ship in disrepair. The Old Testament psalmist in distress
poured out his agony before God, denouncing boldly the
enemy surrounding him. Similarly, a dream of justice allowed
to move into the public consciousness is judgement on
whatever makes it impossible for families to live as families
should—together, with joy in the security of their homes and

without fear of oppression. Dreams are prayers, or pleas,
rooted deep in God's promise for vindication: "Vindicate me,
O God, and plead my cause against an ungodly nation;
rescue me from deceitful and wicked men."

When I think about my future,
what my life is becoming. . .
Profits are small
Each day a small tax to pay.

My father wants money
"We paid for your school
so you could help us."

What is left to hide away
for the woman waiting for me?

Still I will go to the province to teach,
to heal the wounds of war.
I leave my father, my sister, my brother,
though I am the breadwinner.

Maybe when I am very old I will marry,
in my late thirties.
Now I will seek peace while I am still alive.

• *A dreamer is a hope-collector and a hope-bringer.*

A dreamer for peace and justice keeps hope for a better
world alive. It is important to collect dreams for the harmony
of a community if one has experienced injustice and to speak
about those dreams boldly to keep life meaningful.

Therefore, a man or woman with a dream is a lighthouse
to those floundering on the rocks of despair. Martin Luther
King, Jr.'s great dream of a free black people and of all races
living in harmony aroused the spiritual imagination of
thousands of people and invited them to fall in step behind
him with his new call to hope. And they did. Even today,
decades after King's death, to hear the words "I have a

dream" is to hear his clarion call that equality must come for all people.

> Mother, church, husband, house;
> after they took them all
> See, nothing to lose.
> Now I am going to wait
> to see what God will do for me.

> Lydia of Philippi holds me in my dream,
> God helps me get some money.
> Friday I walk to the market
> and gather purple fabric.
> Seven new dresses in six days;
> the women laugh: "Such a small shop!"

> "Little by little the bird makes its nest."

> Now we sit in a circle, one cuts,
> we sew. One prays, we sing.

> Seven women, seventy dresses.

• *Dreams of hope and love create the history of a people.*

John V. Taylor in *Enough Is Enough* (Augsburg) writes that "A culture is an outward expression of the dreams by which the people live." A people's dreams can never by separated from what the people do. The quality of dreams people dream for themselves, for their families, their congregations, their nation, determines what happens, not a rising or falling economy.

"Behind every great achievement is a dreamer of great dreams. Much more than a dreamer is required to bring it to reality; but the dream must be there first," adds Robert K. Greenleaf in *Servant Leadership* (Paulist). Consequently, a dreamer is more powerful in shaping history than the statistician with all the facts.

Hitler had a dream of a nation untainted by blood he considered impure. His dream tore Europe apart and affected nearly every person in the world in some way. Madame Marie Curie had a dream that radium could be developed from pitch-blende and had truckloads of the stuff dumped on her front yard. The pursuit of her dream led to new treatments for cancer. Yes, dreamers are the movers and shakers of the world. Their dreams dangle like a carrot before them, nudging, frustrating, annoying, urging, calling.

> Look over there: that's my house.
> One house, a few bricks.
> See how I worked to build those bricks:
> pull, push, heave, carry.

> Because we are poor,
> I sold more than I kept.
> One house, one bedroom.
> One bedroom, many children.

> We look for water.
> We measure. We dig.
> We find rock.
> We send for a jackhammer.
> We wait a long time.

> When it comes,
> we may find rock.
> Maybe not.

• *Dreamers encourage interdependent relationships between people of all nations.*

If people in other places do not have peace and justice, we do not have peace and justice, for we live in a global village. If we do not work for the fulfillment of others' dreams for peace, we will not have peace. It's as simple as that.

Mennonite Central Committee worker Susan Classen, working in El Salvador, writes out of her trying experiences in that war-torn country that if there is not equal justice in the world and if there are no dreamers of peace and justice, there is the possibility that we, too, will one day be the victims of injustice (*Vultures and Butterflies,* Herald Press, Scottdale, Pennsylvania). Hope will have no home.

Mennonite Central Committee is trying to be that community of hope and love, encouraging dreams and supporting people by walking alongside them, day by day. The support of a community of hope teaches people to dream, for as Jürgen Moltmann writes, "Enduring hope is not something innate, something we possess from birth, nor do we acquire it by experience. We have to learn it."

And we learn to hope "by obeying the call to stand our ground against death and despair. To despair is to give up, to stop trying," writes Classen. The dreamers in this book can teach us to obey that call to keep hope alive.

As you looked at the faces on each page, we hope you saw the invitation there to share their struggle, to be that community of supporters that keeps the dreams voiced in these pictures and words from falling weightless like chaff to the ground. Life's greatest tragedy is to be emptied of dreams and to settle into complacency or despair and darkness. If a dream dies, with it dies a person's sense of aliveness and purpose.

Some of the dreams mentioned in this book are small: "In my dreams I would like to feed my children another meal," "I would like dry shelter," "When I'm grown up, I'd like to wash dishes and clean up for others."

Others have no immediate boundaries and extend over a long period of time: "In my dreams I would like to feed my children for a lifetime," "I wish that we could laugh without being afraid," "In my dreams I would like peace to come to our nation."

Our dreams may be just as small—a roof that doesn't leak when it rains and the pleasure of strolling safe streets at night to watch the stars. And just as large—the cessation of violence on our city streets not only today, but next year also, and the end of hostilities in South Africa, the Baltic countries and Central America. But whether the dreams are large or small, like fishermen, dreamers troll the streets of small villages, large cities, highways and byways, with their nets, looking for people to join the dream movement.

> In my dreams I would like a cow.
> Inside my brick house I and my family
> will look up from our bowls and listen
> to her low contented music after milking.
>
> Through the window we will watch
> the first star climb over her back
> in the violet light.

These faces and voices from seven communities of our world have invited you to face their darkness and despair, to share their struggle, to gain hope from their dreams, but also to add to theirs your own stories of struggle, faith and hope. Adding your story to theirs makes theirs stronger and frees those who have never dared to lift their eyes to thoughts of a brighter future to begin dreaming about the possibilities of something better. Sharing your dream gives your hearers permission "to risk their own dream, knowing that though success may not always follow, the reaching is important" (Katie Funk Wiebe, *Bless Me Too, My Father,* Herald).

Imagine a huge canvas of the world spread before you.

Now on this canvas place all the dreams for righteousness, peace and justice in the world, intricate and beautiful in their own right, yet which bear similarities to one another. Trace the lines connecting one community to another. Let each dream, a small sketch of hope for a better world, together with all the others, come together in a master canvas of God's vision for the earth:

> The Lord will indeed give what is good,
>   and our land will yield its harvest.
> Righteousness goes before him
>   and prepares the way for his steps (Psalm 85:12 NIV).

Next, add your dream of God's community of love and hope to the canvas. Mark it well, for there you stand, at a place of beginning.

Katie Funk Wiebe and Christine R. Wiebe
February 1994

CHRISTINE R. WIEBE is a freelance writer and nurse. A former Mennonite Central Committee volunteer, she has also been involved in a Catholic Worker community and worked as a city parish nurse. Currently she directs a free nurses' clinic for homeless and low-income people at Venture House, an Episcopal Social Service agency in Wichita, Kansas.

KATIE FUNK WIEBE is professor emeritus of English at Tabor College, Hillsboro, Kansas, where she taught for 24 years. A freelance writer and editor, she has written or edited 12 books in addition to numerous study and devotional guides and hundreds of articles. She has traveled widely and currently lives in Wichita, Kansas.

AFTERWORD

This book is based on a simple premise: photographs can be a powerful link between people. They can contribute to a sense of community by introducing people and by highlighting connections.

But is this really true?

We know photographs can be powerful. Nick Ut's famous photograph of a terrified Vietnamese girl running toward the camera after a napalm attack helped turn the tide in the United States against the Vietnam war. That photograph of war's terror is implanted in the memory of a whole generation.

Today, though, we are so flooded with images that the power of individual photos seems quite diluted. The trivial and the profound, the silly and the tragic, all come at us in a blur. The important becomes banal. The horrific has become commonplace, raising our tolerance of what is abhorrent. Do photographs still have power to affect us?

As proof that they do, I offer a simple test. Think of some memory: say from childhood, say of a happy moment, perhaps even something that frightened you. Chances are you are seeing an image in your mind. Chances are, in fact, that you are seeing a still image, not a moving image— a photo, not a movie. Photographer Galen Rowell has suggested that if still images are this basic, the building blocks of memory and feeling, then photography remains a powerful means of communication.

Too often, though, photographs serve to divide rather than connect. They emphasize the "otherness" of subjects. They leave subjects feeling degraded and violated. They undermine rather than build a sense of community.

Photography can exploit or it can respect. Its impact depends on how it is conducted. That, in turn, is determined in subtle, often unconscious ways, by how we talk and think about what we do when we photograph. How we do photography is affected by how we view photography, and that in turn is affected by the images and metaphors that shape our language.

When we think and talk about concepts or, in fact, anything that we cannot see or touch, we compare them to other things. Consequently, most of our ideas about the world are couched in images and metaphors.

When we talk about justice, we "right" wrongs or "weigh the evidence," using the image of a scale. The Bible uses many metaphors to talk about God; God is described as an eagle, a shepherd, light, a fortress, a woman giving birth, a father . . . the list could go on. In such cases, we are using something we understand to comprehend and symbolize something we know incompletely.

Our metaphors subtly shape how we see and react to the world. When we talk about a "war on crime," for example, we are using the metaphor of battle to describe a social problem. This metaphor in turn reinforces certain stereotypes and assumptions. It emphasizes the "otherness" of offenders,

disguising the fact that they are very much like us; as the Bible frequently reminds us, we are all offenders. By objectifying an "enemy," the war metaphor allows us to justify all sorts of actions against offenders. This metaphor creates the false impression that the solution lies in weapons, in "outgunning" the enemy, in deterrence through fear.

In photography, the words and metaphors we use are profoundly disturbing. We shoot or take a photo. We aim our camera. Often we approach photography like a hunt, stealing photos without the consent of the subject and collecting images like trophies.

This militaristic image is reflected in the design and use of equipment. Cameras with their protruding lenses often look like weapons, then we put them in front of our faces like masks or guns. And they are advertised this way. A famous lens manufacturer announces that its "new snub-nose zoom shoots to kill." An ad for a photo lab has a cowboy holding a camera like a gun against a western sky with a "wanted" poster on the wall behind him. A store for professional photographers advertises that the company is "responsible for over 2,876,431 shootings." It touts its "arsenal" of equipment and promises that their service will "blow you away."

The language of photography is predominately aggressive, predatory, acquisitive, imperialistic. The camera is imaged as a weapon.

The way we actually do photography, unfortunately, all too often reflects this image of photographer-as-aggressor. We steal photos with a telephoto lens without the subject's consent. We use the camera to avoid interacting with our subjects. We treat the photos as commodities with no input from the subjects about how they are portrayed, how the image is edited or where it is used.

Is it any surprise, then, that subjects feel violated and that photos so often divide and degrade?

The photographs in this book are based on an alternative image of photography.

When we photograph, we do not actually reach out and take anything. Rather, we receive an image that is reflected from the subject. Instead of understanding photography as *taking* then, we can envision it as *receiving*. Instead of a trophy that is hunted, an image is a gift.

In reality, photography is a matter of opening ourselves to receiving. Such photography means cultivating a receptive attitude, an openness to the unexpected. Such photography is more like meditation than a hunt.

Conceived in this way, photography requires respect for the subject. The subject—whether landscape or person—plays a crucial part in our creation and so it becomes a collaborative effort, an exchange. As photographer John Running says in his book *Pictures for Solomon*, "Making a photograph is usually a collaboration between the photographer and the subject. It doesn't matter if the subject is a landscape, a still life, an animal or a person." As a result, he says, he tries to photograph "with care, respect, truth and wonder."

So there is an alternative to the photographer-as-aggressor image. Instead of imagining photography as taking, we can understand it as receiving a gift; we can approach it as a collaboration, an exchange.

Only when we photograph with care, respect, truth and wonder can we create photographs that build rather than destroy life-giving community.

Howard Zehr
March 1994

The proceeds from the sale of this book will go to the work of Mennonite Central Committee, the relief, service and development agency of the Mennonite and Brethren in Christ churches in Canada and the United States, thanks to the generosity of these people in underwriting the costs of producing this publication:

Friesen Printers
Lehman Hardware and Appliances, Inc.
Ontario Donors
Henry and Charlotte Rosenberger
A Saskatchewan Donor
United Service Foundation
David and Lorma Wiebe